An Examination Into The Genuineness Of The Jeannette Relics: Some Evidences Of Currents In The Polar Region

The Geographical Society Of The Pacific

In the interest of creating a more extensive selection of rare historical book reprints, we have chosen to reproduce this title even though it may possibly have occasional imperfections such as missing and blurred pages, missing text, poor pictures, markings, dark backgrounds and other reproduction issues beyond our control. Because this work is culturally important, we have made it available as a part of our commitment to protecting, preserving and promoting the world's literature. Thank you for your understanding.

The Geographical Society of the Pacific.

An Examination into the Genuineness of the "Jeannette" Relics.

Some Evidences of Currents in the Polar Regions.

REPORT OF THE SPECIAL COMMITTEE APPOINTED BY THE COUNCIL TO REPORT UPON THE "JEANNETTE" RELICS.

SAN FRANCISCO:
John Partridge, Printer and Publisher, 42-44 Steuart St.
1896

OFFICERS

PRESIDENT
PROFESSOR GEORGE DAVIDSON, Ph. D., Sc. D.

VICE-PRESIDENTS
HON. RALPH C. HARRISON   IRVING M. SCOTT
CHAS. L. TAYLOR

DIRECTORS
PROF. GEO. DAVIDSON   E. J. BOWEN
HARRY DURBROW   L. L. NELSON
CHAS. L. TAYLOR   JOHN DOLBEER
JOHN PARTRIDGE

TREASURER
HARRY DURBROW

HOME CORRESPONDING SECRETARY
HON. JEREMIAH LYNCH

FOREIGN CORRESPONDING SECRETARY
MARK SHELDON

RECORDING SECRETARY
JOHN PARTRIDGE

ASSISTANT SECRETARY
T. F. TRENOR, M. A.

COUNCIL
HON. CHAS. GOODALL   HON. JEREMIAH LYNCH
MARK SHELDON   IRVING M. SCOTT
HON. RALPH C. HARRISON   GUSTAVE NIEBAUM
WM. HOOD, C. E.   HENRY LUND
HON. GEO. C. PERKINS   Consul for Sweden and Norway
JAS. F. HOUGHTON   F. STEVENS COOK, M. D.
HON. ADOLPH SUTRO, Mayor of San Francisco

LIBRARY AND OFFICE OF THE SOCIETY
MERCHANTS EXCHANGE BUILDING

LIEUTENANT GEORGE W. DE LONG, U. S. N., COMMANDER "JEANNETTE."

THE "JEANNETTE" WAS ORIGINALLY "HER BRITTANIC MAJESTY'S SHIP 'PANDORA,' WHICH WAS SOLD IN 1872 TO SIR ALLEN YOUNG (THE ARCTIC EXPLORER), FROM WHOM MR. JAMES GORDON BENNETT BOUGHT HER IN JANUARY, 1878."

The Committee begs to make the following Report:

Upon the recent news from the interior of Siberia that Dr. Nansen's expedition had returned to the north coast of Siberia, several persons publicly expressed their views upon the probability of the report being true; and expressed their opinions of the theory upon which Dr. Nansen had undertaken his attempt to cross the Polar basin by means of the currents carrying his vessel when jammed in the ice. His theory was mainly based upon the evidences of Polar currents, favorable to his project and more especially upon the finding of the relics of the "Jeannette" in 1884.

When these relics were found the interest of this Society was at once aroused, the more especially as some of the articles belonged to San Francisco; and Dr. Th. E. Slevin, our First Vice-President, was authorized to open correspondence with the Danish Governor of Greenland to obtain some of them; but the line of communication was so long and irregular that our efforts finally ceased until 1894, when Mr. Lund visited Copenhagen and learned how the relics had been lost. His report in detail has been presented to the Society, and while we regretted the loss of these valuable evidences of the movement of the Polar currents we did not lose our faith in the genuineness of the relics.

But doubt has been cast upon their being genuine by Dr. W. H. Dall of the U. S. Geological Survey, Washington, in several newspaper interviews wherein he is reported to have said that the relics as found were the result of a trick played by some persons of the U. S. Greely relief expeditions of 1883 and 1884; and moreover, that he had communicated the facts of such trickery to Dr. Nansen. These are very important statements in more ways than one, because they involve the integrity of the United States Navy Officers, and would, if true, indicate very loose discipline.

In the National Geographic Magazine of March, 1896, Dr. Dall has made his statement upon "the so-called 'Jeannette' "Relics." This mode of designation has a peculiar and unfavorable significance in American literature. After explaining the former newspaper interviews Dr. Dall enters upon an extended explanation that during the Government investigations of 1885 and relates that Dr. Emil Bessels, of his own account and without any direction of the proper authorities, interviewed some of the seamen as well as their officers; and that he obtained 40 or 50 pages of evidence "tending to support

" his hypothesis that some person or persons unknown had 'in
" a spirit of boyish levity' perpetrated the hoax of placing the
" relics upon an ice-floe and thereby 'producing a sensation in
" the fleet.'" Dr. Dall "was present at one or two interviews."

How the placing of these articles on an ice-floe that would never be visited by any one of the fleet could produce a sensation among them, is clearly illogical; had such articles been found by the fleet, a searching inquiry would surely have resulted in conviction and punishment of the culprits as they must well have known.

If the language of Dr. Dall's statement No. 5 be carefully read, it will be seen that Dr. Bessels was gathering evidence to support a hypothesis that the articles could not have been preserved so long; that these 40 or 50 foolscap pages at most "tended to support this hypothesis" and that no "particular " man questioned was personally cognizant of the act." And yet "Dr. Bessels communicated to his European correspondents " his belief that the relics were fictitious and the result of " hoax," and Dr. Dall "stated to Dr. Rink and others who " inquired of me the same conclusions." Why Dr. Bessels and Dr. Dall did not make this matter known to the Government while so important an investigation was going on is matter for further explanation. It would be interesting to learn why no Geographical Society was made aware of the doubts of Dr. Bessels. So far as we can learn the American Geographical Society did not hear of the doubts. And it is unfortunate that the Bessels evidence, like the "Jeannette" relics, met with destruction.

In statement No. 6 Dr. Dall continues: " In 1888 Dr. Nansen " made his celebrated journey across Greenland and presumably " heard of the relics there. Up to this time either the doubts " which had been thrown on the authenticity of the relics, or " some other reason, had prevented them exciting much interest, " and the owner seems to have resisted any attempt to verify their " authenticity by sending photographs or originals of the papers " to America when requested." It would be strange if Dr. Nansen had not made exhaustive inquiries about them had he been informed of the doubts expressed by Dr. Bessels. So far as we can learn he has not made himself accessory after the fact to such a fraud by withholding knowledge upon the subject. The relics were the property of the Royal Geographical Society of Copenhagen, and the reputation of that body was at stake in the finding and character of the relics. What Dr. Nansen has said about the relics is found in the proceedings of the meeting of the Royal Geographical Society of London, held January, 1893, where the ablest Arctic navigators and explorers were assembled to hear him, to offer advice and to criticize him freely. In referring to some doubts which had been expressed of the genuineness of the relics he stated that a well known American traveler had maintained that if the relics were found it would seem reasonable to trace them to the "Proteus" which had been wrecked in Smith Sound 1,000 miles north of Julianshaab in July, 1883. He did not refer to any communication from Dr. Bessels or Dr. Dall. He mentioned that the articles were sent to the International Exhibition at Amsterdam; how he had sought to see them, and that he arrived at Copenhagen two months after their destruction. Then he showed how they must have come down the east coast of Greenland by well-known historical examples of drifting and by his own experience.

Dr. Dall says of that meeting that "the doubtful character of "the so-called 'Jeannette' relics was also distinctly pointed "out." The term "so-called" was not applied to the relics and the strongest expression of opinion was afterward written out by Admiral Sir George H. Richards as follows: "If the "'Jeannette' articles were found in Greenland they may well "have drifted down on a floe from the neighborhood of "Smith's Sound from some of the American expeditions which "went to Greely's rescue. It may also well be that some of "the 'De Long's' printed or written documents, in regard to "his equipment, may have been taken out by these expedi-"tions, and the same may apply to the other articles" [of the Franklin rescue expeditions]. The explanation is simply puerile, and the insinuation that "the written documents may have "been taken out by these expeditions," is a serious charge against our navy officers. We cannot wonder that Dr. Nansen gave no heed to such evidence.

Before Dr. Nansen started on his last expedition Dr. Dall says that "a friend wrote to me on Nansen's behalf for my opin-"ion in this matter, which was sent before Nansen started." The letter and the friend's name are not recalled by Dr. Dall. "Baron Nordenskjöld was also informed sometime before "Nansen sailed, so there is no doubt that Nansen was cog-"nizant of the fact that the authenticity of the relics was ser-"iously questioned."

It is therefore very desirable that Baron Nordenskjöld present some explanation. Dr. Dall then states his "conclusions: It is "evident that the proof that the relics were the result of a hoax "is not complete, and in the nature of things, unless the par-"ties actually concerned shall admit it, is never likely to be "completed." And yet he occupies two more pages in the vain effort to prove that the articles could never have been brought to Greenland by Polar currents

The Committee will soon refer to this matter of currents.

General Greely in the same number of the magazine (p 99 says: "The drift relics found on the west coast of Greenland " * * * were relied upon by Nansen as practical proof "that his theory of a drift voyage was correct; but that [Chief

"Engineer] Melville, the man best qualified to speak about
"the 'Jeannette,' denied at the time their genuineness, and
"endeavored without avail to have them brought to this
"country." Why Melville was so qualified is not mentioned;
The Bank of California and Capt. S. B. Peterson of San Francisco could vouch for very important papers, as we shall presently show. Gen. Greely further says that he "publicly
"called Nansen's attention to this question, which for the first
"time seems to have created doubts in his mind. Nanson
"made efforts to find the relics for verification, but they had
"disappeared in toto," as we have already mentioned.

General Greely is far from sanguine about the success of Nansen's expedition. He says that "if Nansen really ap-
"proached the Pole before his vessel was destroyed, it is safe
"to say that he will pay for an unequalled latitude with his
"life and carry the secret of his well-earned success to the
"grave." We have faith that Nansen will return safely, whatever be the spot where he will strike the shores of the Polar basin.

As Dr. Dall has referred to the drift of the spear-throwing stick and the Siberian pine in a deprecatory way, we propose to refer to these and to evidences of other drifts.

THE ARCTIC DRIFTS.

1—THE DRIFT OF H. B. M. SHIP "RESOLUTE."

The British discovery ships "Intrepid" and "Resolute," two of Sir Edward Belcher's expedition, were abandoned August 26th, 1854, when frozen in South of Bathurst Land, in the eastern part of Melville Sound in lat. 74° 40' north, and long. 101° 25' west. The "Resolute" was found derelict by Captain Buddington of the American whaler "George Henry" on the 11th of September, 1855, on the west side of the northern part of Davis Strait, 80 miles south by west from Cape Washington, in lat. 64° 40' north, and long. 61° 30' west. By the shortest route possible, through Melville Sound, the narrow, island-barred Barrow Strait and Baffin's Bay into Davis Strait, she must have drifted 1,100 nautical miles in 381 days.

2—THE DRIFT OF THE ICE-FLOE WITH THE "POLARIS" PEOPLE.

On the night of October 15th, 1872, the U. S. S. "Polaris," then commanded by Capt. O. S. Budington, successor to Capt. Chas. F. Hall, was badly nipped in the ice in Smith Strait, and the records, some of the provisions, and part of the officers, crew and all the Esquimaux, were removed to an ice-floe preparatory to abandoning the ship. This floe separated from the ship off Cape Ohlsen in lat. 78° 25' north, and long. 73° 25' west, and part of it drifted southward with nineteen persons upon it. Fortunately the Assistant Navigator of the "Polaris," Captain George E. Tyson, was upon this floe, and all the nine Esquimaux, who were good hunters.

On the 30th of April, 1873, after incredible hardships, this party was rescued by the steam whaling barkentine "Tigress" Captain Bartlett of Conception Bay, Newfoundland, about 50 miles east of Grady Harbor, Labrador, in lat. 53° 35' north, and long. 55° 00' west (both approximate). This ice-floe had made a drift of about 1,700 miles to the southward and eastward in 197 days, or an average of over 8 miles per day.

3—THE DRIFT OF THE SPEAR-THROWING STICK.

Dr. Dall refers to the finding of the Alaskan spear-throwing stick of the Port Clarence Esquimaux in order to discredit its having reached Greenland by drifting through Arctic waters. Per contra, Dr. Nansen cites the incident to confirm the current movement of those waters. From the peculiar shape and the particular glassbead ornamentation of this throwing stick, its locality has been fixed with certainty to the region of Port Clarence, Norton Sound, on the Alaskan side just south of Bering Strait. It was found near Godthaab, on the west coast of Greenland in latitude 64°, and is now in the ethnological museum of Christiania. Dr. Dall suggests that some seaman of a whaler carried this unattractive curio from Port Clarence, and conjecturally to Greenland. It is a thousand times more likely that it was carried through Bering Strait northward and thence through the very channel which the "Resolute" followed.

4—THE DRIFT OF THE SIBERIAN PINE.

Dr. Dall refers to the drift of the Siberian pine, but gives it little or no weight. Admiral Sir E. Englefield whom he quotes, thinks differently. At the meeting of the Royal Geographical Society of London, where Nansen explained his project, his methods and the proofs of the currents upon which he relied, Admiral Englefield said: "I can give Dr. Nansen a word of en-
" couragement by telling him that on my second voyage I walked
" up one shore of Wellington Sound to meet Sir Edward Bel-
" cher, and one evening we were in luck in finding a pine tree
" one foot in diameter and about 15 to 16 feet long with the
" bark upon it, and very little bruised. We know it can have
" come from no other part of the world but Siberia. A portion
" of the bark was brought home and the naturalist, with his
" microscope, discovered seed and matter which assured him
" that it had not been more than a few months in the water.
" This was on the western side of Wellington Sound," which enters Barrow Strait just 130 miles east of where the "Intre-

pid" and "Resolute" were abandoned. The tree may have come in from the northwestard direct from the Arctic through the short Penny Strait, sixteen hundred miles from the Siberian Coast, or from the westward through Melville Sound.

Admiral Englefield's remarks were followed by Sir Allen Young, who said: "I believe there can be no doubt that the "relics from the 'Jeannette' were genuine, and must have "drifted on the floe upon which they were thrown when the "ship was abandoned; and could come to the Greenland coast "in the time by no other way but across the Pole or nearly so. "These 'Jeannette' relics may have drifted through narrow "channels and thus finally arrived at their destination;" but he adds that "it would be an extremely dangerous thing for a "ship to drift through them."

5—THE MOVEMENT OF SIBERIAN DRIFTWOOD AND OTHER MATERIAL.

Dr. Dall points to the enormous number of over one hundred wrecks in Greenland waters, of which not a single relic has ever been recognized, but admits that driftwood from northern rivers is cast upon the coast every year. The first assertion needs verification, to be obtained only from the natives. We cannot take it for granted. Dr. Nansen has adduced the driftwood as evidence in his favor, and has shown that there is much drift-wood from Siberia, and perhaps from the American Arctic coast which reaches Greenland every year. He says: "This wood is generally Siberian larch and red spruce, and I "have examined a great deal of it on the west and east coast "of Greenland, and have found it floating on the sea among "the floe ice near Jan Mayen and Spitzbergen. Its appearance "indicated that it had not been long in the water. This drift "wood is a necessity for the Greenland Esquimaux for wea- "pons, implements, boats, sledges, tents, etc. Without it "they would be in great distress.

"It is found in Spitzbergen, especially on the northern "shores, and also in the sea north of this land and among the "ice-floes carried southward from the unknown north.

"Samples of dust and mud found on the ice-floes between "Iceland and Greenland are believed by geologist Dr. "Törnebohm to come from the Siberian lands and rivers."

"Even the diatom flora on ice-floes near Bering Sound "and on the east coast of Greenland are so completely alike, "and so unlike all others that this fact indicates an open com- "munication between the seas east of Greenland and the north "of Asia."

He gives his own experience on the west and east coasts of Greenland in 1882 and 1888, and notes the enormous thickness of the ice that drifts down the east coast as evidence of it coming from an area of intense cold, such as exists north of Siberia.

6—THE DRIFT OF THE "FOX," THE "HANSA" AND THE "WHALING FLEET OF 1777."

Dr. Nansen called the attention of the old Arctic explorers to "Sir Leopold McClintock's drift with the 'Fox' during eight "months in the winter of 1857-58, when he was carried 1200 "miles from the northern part of Baffin's Bay down toward "Labrador.

"The whole fleet of whalers (about 28) which in June, 1777, "were nipped between lats. 74° and 75° N. drifted in the "ice southward along the east Greenland Coast. The last "ship was crushed in October in lat. 61° 30' N. after having "drifted 1250 miles in 107 days. Some of the men continued "the drift on the ice. rounded Cape Farewell and reached at "last the Danish settlements on the west coast; their whole "drift being about 1600 miles."

Then he mentioned the drift of the "Hansa" over the same course in 1869 70 in nine months. On the other hand Dr. Dall indirectly casts some doubt upon this current rounding Cape Farewell by questioning its equal strength at all seasons, and thinks that along such a coast as Greenland eddies and reverse currents cannot fail to occur.

7—CURRENTS THROUGH THE CHANNELS OF THE ARCTIC ISLANDS WEST OF GREENLAND.

Among the islands from Greenland to the Mackenzie river there are six channels through which Nansen's vessel might pass. We have through three of them the drift of the "Polaris" ice-floe, the "Siberian Pine," and the "Resolute." It has been demonstrated by the drift of the "Resolute" through McClure Strait that the current runs to the eastward, and our whalers who have wintered at Herschel Island for several winters' past have found a very strong current setting into the Strait between Cape Kellett and Cape Bathurst, about 240 miles westward of McClure Strait. Both of these straits evidently receive waters in part from the western Arctic shore of Alaska, or from the Arctic Ocean to the westward and northward. Dr. Nansen considers the east Greenland current carries such an immense volume of water that it must drain the Polar basin by drawing the water from the Siberian Coast, and even from Bering Strait. The movement of the Polar current from the Bering Strait militates with former papers of Dr. Dall in which he endeavored to prove the current through that strait was to the southward. Dr. Nansen says that "all (American) expeditions (through Smith Sound) were "effectually stopped by the floe ice carried down by a current "from the north."

EVIDENCE CONCERNING THE "JEANNETTE" RELICS.

The Committee now proposes to recall one or two incidents of the loss of the "Jeannette," and present some evidence from an American captain who saw the relics soon after they were found, and from one of the survivors of the "Jeannette."

The "Jeannette" left San Francisco July 8th, 1879, in company with a vessel chartered at this port to carry much of her material to St. Michaels or to some port in Bering Sea south of lat. 68°.

On Friday, Sept. 5th, 1879, she entered the ice pack in the vicinity of Wrangell Land, and soon after became fixed in the floe and thence drifted to the northward and westward with the pack until she was crushed and sank in 38 fathoms of water at 4 A. M. Monday, June 13th, 1881, in lat. 77° 15' north, and 154° 59' east.

While the vessel was in jeopardy ample time was given to prepare for the retreat of the officers and crew with boats, sleds, stores, clothing, instruments, etc., which were placed upon an adjacent ice-floe. All the clothing that was not in use was placed in a common heap, and each person by direction of Captain De Long, took whatever he choose for one suit, and one suit of underclothing to be carried in his knapsack. Mrs. Emma De Long (Vol. 11, page 578) says there were 170 pieces left on the floe after the five or six days spent in preparation of the sleds, boats and stores. The retreat was commenced over the ice June 18th, 1881.

Everything was abandoned that was not absolutely necessary for the safety of the party. Of the six tents that were put on the floe five were party tents and one was an office tent. Five tents only were carried on the sleds according to Noros' account. We need not follow the heroic and terrible struggles of the officers and men.

On Friday, August fifteenth, 1884, the American bark "Fluorine," Capt. Alexander Wilson, arrived at Philadelphia from Ivigtut, the port of shipment of the Kryolite mines a few miles northwestward from Julianshaab. It is on the southwest coast of Greenland about 110 miles northwest from Cape Farewell. The "Fluorine" brought the following official communication from the Danish Colonial Governor of Greenland to the Danish Consul at New York:

"The Colony Julianshaab, in South Greenland, June 23rd. 1884.

"To the Consul for Denmark at New York—

"I hereby take the liberty to request the Consulate to inform "the editors of the *New York Herald* that on the 18th inst. "three Greenlanders picked up on an ice-floe some effects and "some partly torn papers belonging to the American Arctic "'Jeannette' Expedition, among which are the following:

"1.—Two end-pieces of a wooden box, on which are written
"with lead pencil on one piece—

General Orders	*Ships Papers*
Telegrams	*Various Agreements*
Sailing Orders	*Charter Party*

"the last words not very plain.

"2.—On the other piece was—

Before Sailing

"3.—A town check book. On the back of one of the checks
"is printed, 'For Deposit with the Bank of California.'
"4.—A pair of oilskin trousers, marked, 'Louis Noros.'
"These effects, numbering twenty-one pieces (besides the
"papers), are in my possession. I am going home to remain
"during the winter   Should anybody want further informa-
"tion, the same can obtain it by addressing—
"Kolonibestyrer C. Lytzen,
"Kongl. Grönl. Handels-Kontor,
"Kjöbnhavn. K.,
"Denmark.
"Respectfully, Carl Lytzen."

Immediately upon receipt of this information at San Francisco, Mr. Chas. W. Brooks of the California Academy of Sciences wrote to Captain Wilson at Philadelphia, who furnished him with the following statement: (Geographical Society of the Pacific publication September 2nd. 1884.)
"The Superintendent of the Kryolite mines at Ivigtut first
"informed him of this highly important discovery. A party
"of Esquimaux were out among the floe ice catching seal.
"Late in the afternoon of Wednesday, June 18th, 1884, they
"approached a large piece of ice which had attracted their
"attention, (floating in lat. 60° 36′ north, longitude 46° 07′
"west), upon which they found the lower part of a tent. the
"upper part of which had been blown away by storms; also
"the end of a provision cask, and some stores marked
"'Jeannette;' a charter party 'between S. B. Peterson, man-
"aging owner of the American schooner 'Fanny A. Hyde,'
"Capt. J. W. Peterson, of San Francisco, California, and
"George W. De Long, from Mare Island Navy Yard, to the
"port of St. Michaels in Norton Sound, Territory of Alaska,
"U. S. A., there for delivery to the Arctic steamer

"'Jeannette;' also a partially used check book on the Bank
"of California, with a package of cancelled checks, signed by
"Capt. De Long; a pair of oil skin trousers marked 'Louis
"Noros,' and a bear skin covering something of the size and
"shape of a human corpse, which the Greenlanders did not
"remove to ascertain what was under it, owing to a native
"superstition rendering those temporarily unclean who
"handle the dead bodies of human beings.

"On another piece of floe near by, quite a quantity of
"sailors' clothing was found. These relics the Esquimaux
"took to the Governor of Julianshaab, who immediately
"started, taking one of their number as a guide, to find the
"ice-floe and the supposed body; but it had floated away."

Capt. Wilson "believes that what the bear skin covered was
"only apparently in shape that of a human body. It may
"have been a long water breaker of which some were carried
"by the 'Jeannette' from the Mare Island Navy Yard."

On the 20th of August, 1884, Louis Phillipe Noros, one of
the survivors, wrote to Mr. Brooks from Newburyport as follows: "Before we left the 'Jeannette' we carried on to the
"ice a lot of bearskins, which we spread out to form a floor,
"and in addition carried clothing, food, rifles, tobacco, etc.
"After the 'Jeannette' was crushed we had to leave the bear-
"skins, a lot of canned goods, cans, rifles, and 200 or 300
"pounds of tobacco behind, as we could not carry them all
"over the ice. We also left all the clothing except what we
"had on, and a suit of underclothing which we packed and
"carried in a knapsack. We carried five tents with us, De
"Long's party having two, Melville's two, and Chip's one. I
"may possibly have left my sealskin [oilskin?] pantaloons on
"the ice where the 'Jeannette' went down, but my impression
"is that they were left with the other clothing, ships imple-
"ments, utensils, papers, etc., in the cache left by De Long on
"the Siberian coast. We had four tin boxes, in which De
"Long kept the ship's log and valuable papers, two of
"which were left in the cache and two carried away by De
"Long when Quartermaster Windermann and I started south
"for help. We also left in the cache a small bearskin, the
"only bearskin in the possession of the party after leaving the
"'Jeannette.' The account says that a cask of miscellaneous
"ship provisions was found marked 'Jeannette' Now the
"fact is, we did take some bread barrels out, but after
"putting the bread in bags and loading it on our sleds we left
"the empty barrels behind on the ice."

Noros further states: "What puzzled me most is how these
"articles now reported found could have remained on the ice
"so long. My experience taught me that all small articles
"placed on the ice in the Arctic region always attracted the
"sun and gradually melted down through the ice until lost to

"sight. Why, in a very short time a chip would be buried
"its own thickness by this peculiar power, and if the things
"found really belonged to the 'Jeannette' something strangely
"wonderful seems to have providentially kept them so long
"a time on the face of the ice."

This letter accounts for one tent abandoned on the ice-floe and its remains found in the ice, and it accounts for the presence of a bear skin from among the many that were left on the floe.

THE CHARTER PARTY AND THE CHECK-BOOK.

Dr. Dall states that the relics were sent by Herr Lytzen to a friend in Copenhagen; we understand they were sent to the Royal Geographical Society of Copenhagen, who became the custodians. Among them he mentions "especially a list of the "boats of the 'Jeannette' and a list of provisions signed by "De Long," leaving the inference that these were the most important articles recovered.

We more especially call attention to the charter party and the partially used check-book on the Bank of California with a package of cancelled checks not referred to by Dr. Dall. This charter party is marked on the end of the box, and we have traced up and present the following facts relating to this paper. Capt. S. B. Peterson has shown us the copy of this paper, which was executed by himself and George W. De Long. It was "made and concluded upon in San Francisco on the seventh "day of July in the year of our Lord one thousand eight hun- "dred and seventy-nine, between S. P. Peterson, managing "owner of the American schooner 'Fanny A. Hyde,' etc.," but it does not mention the name of Capt. J. W. Jesperson, which was stated by Capt. Wilson to be on the charter party found on the ice-floe. Nor does another copy in the possession of the Alaska Commercial Company of San Francisco show his name Capt. Gustav Niebaum says that Capt. De Long was in a great hurry to obtain a vessel to carry his coal, etc., and that he (Niebaum) fortunately found the "Fanny A. Hyde" for him. Capt. Peterson informs us he quickly selected Capt. J. W. Jesperson to command her because he was a skillful seaman, and he sent a good navigator, L. P. Larsen, as mate. The bill of lading, as shown in duplicate, in the possession of the Alaska Commercial Co., was signed by J. W. Jesperson as the commanding officer. It is therefore probable that Capt. De Long either put Jesperson's name on the outer indorsement of the charter party or that he attached the bill of lading to it. Hence the mention of both names by Capt. Wilson.

Mr. Thomas Brown, the Cashier of the Bank of California, has given us a full statement of Capt. De Long's bank account which commenced on the 4th of June and closed July 8th, the day of his departure, after which his accounts were attended to by the Alaska Commercial Company. De Long had drawn twenty-five checks, which were cancelled and returned to him.

We ask seriously: Is it within the reach of probability that a sailor (presumably Louis Noros, from a suggestive remark by Dr. Dall) would carry these articles and the papers through the dangers on the ice trip, thence to the Siberian coast, and through all the hardships of that frightful struggle on shore, to put them on an ice-floe in Davis Strait or Baffin's Bay in the bare possibility of " producing a sensation in the fleet?" And with the papers all the other articles declared to have been recovered? And how was Noros or Winderman to know when they left that ice-floe in the Arctic that they would ever be in Baffin's Bay?

THE SUBSCRIBERS TO THE NANSEN EXPEDITION.

There is, however, another consideration not heretofore referred to, which shows the strong faith which Dr. Nansen and his government and scientific and commercial friends had in the proof of the movement of the Polar currents, and that is, the amount of money which they subscribed toward the outfit of the expedition including insurance and wages up to June 18th, 1896.

	Crowns at 27c.
Personal subscription from H. M. Oscar II, and sundry private parties, including Professor Nordenskjöld and Baron Dickson	135,237.58
Contribution from the Norwegian Government,	280,000.00
Accrued interest thereon	3,839.28
Dr. Nansen	7,862.50
Guaranteed by private parties	5,400.00
Deficiency made up by Consul A. Heiberg and Mr. A. Dick, merchant	12,000.00
Crowns	444,339.36
Or in gold coin	$119,971.63

And it should be further noted that the Norwegian Storthing [Parliament] has voted [1896] a large amount to provide for further wages and insurance for the crew of the "Fram" and for the care of their families.

Nordenskjöld and Nansen had heard the rumors of doubt about the relics, and is it likely that they would have placed their own money in this venture and have obtained the assistance of the King, of Baron Dickson and of the government, if they had any reasonable doubt of their genuineness? Had they believed in such a unique fraud would they have made themselves accessory after the fact to such a premeditated, wicked act, committed by men of the United States Navy under the very eyes of alert officers? Moreover, before these moneys were subscribed for the Nansen Expedition of 1893 a chart of the circumpolar regions was published at Christiania and freely circulated. It exhibited the possible Arctic route and the probable East Greenland route of the 'Jeannette' relics; and the possible Polar route of Dr. Nansen from North Cape along the Arctic coast to the mouths of the Lena river; thence northeastward to the vicinity af Bennett Island in latitude 77½ deg. north, and longitude 150 deg. east. From this position he supposed his vessel, when jammed in the ice, would be carried nearly northward to the vicinity of the Pole, and thence to the northeastern part of Greenland about latitude 85 deg., whence the currents to the southward flow with constant but slow and irresistible force, as we have already shown. He hoped to be out of the ice-floe of this current in about 70 deg. latitude and two or three hundred miles off the east coast of Greenland. Professor H. Mohr examined this chart carefully and paid especial attention to the location of the known warm and cold currents. The data upon this chart have not, so far as we have learned, been controverted.

There is of course a probability of the drift across the Polar region carrying the ice-floe more directly to the north shores and channels of the islands west of Greenland, and spreading largely therefrom toward the eastward. It was, however, the eddy current running northwestard along the southwestern Greenland shore from Cape Farewell that decided Nansen and his friends in their belief that the relics followed the east shore of Greenland from the polar region. This inside eddy shore drift bringing its ice-floes into the west side of Davis Strait, is believed to be sufficiently strong and persistent to prevent ice-floes from Baffin's Bay reaching the southwest shore; and in consequence should have prevented any ice-floes carrying Dr. Dall's so-called 'Jeannette' relics from the United States relief fleet at the north to the coast near Julianshaab.

And in conclusion the Committee beg to recall Mr. Lund's visit to Copenhagen and his report upon the "Jeannette" relics.

Upon the recent request of the Society concerning his visit to Copenhagen in 1894, Mr. Henry Lund, Consul at San Francisco for Sweden and Norway, has answered briefly the result of his mission. He had previously read an extended paper upon the relics, their discovery and their destruction, having been authorized by this Society to purchase some of the articles, especially those relating to San Francisco. After expressing surprise at the statements of Dr. Dall, he says: " In " June, 1894, I met Commodore Otto Irminger of the Royal " Geographical Society of Copenhagen, and in our conference " he informed me that much to the regret of the Society and " all parties concernned, it was impossible to find any of the " relics. They had been given into the charge of a member " whom they considered a perfectly safe custodian who had " placed them in the garret of his dwelling. This person died, "and when, some time afterwards other people moved into the "house, they had it cleaned up and the rubbish removed by "scavengers to the dump hills. Among this rubbish were the "relics, so unsuggestive, that any one unacquainted with their "history would naturally consider them of no value. The "Society of Copenhagen only missed them some time after "when our Society was seeking to purchase some of them. It "was then too late to recover them, and Commodore Irminger "said nothing remained but to express profound regret." And further, Mr. Lund says it would be strange if Governor Lytzen should have allowed himself to be imposed upon, and that the Royal Geographical Society of Copenhagen should have published detailed accounts of the discovery and relics unless satisfied of their genuineness.

After carefully weighing these statements, and recalling the mental and physical characteristics of Dr. Nansen and the brave comrades and men who cheerfully accompany him, and the special fitness of the "Fram" to encounter ice dangers, the Committee places upon record its convictions—that the present expedition was fully warranted, and that it will return successful.

Respectfully submitted,

GEORGE DAVIDSON,
HENRY LUND,
Committee.

THE GEOGRAPHICAL SOCIETY OF THE PACIFIC.
San Francisco, Cal., May 9th, 1896.

At the special meeting of the Council held May 12th, the Report of the Committee upon the "Jeannette" Relics was adopted and ordered printed.

Put to press June 3, 1896.

Printed by Libri Plureos GmbH in Hamburg, Germany